HOW TO CREATE DIGITAL PORTFOLIOS TO DEVELOP COMMUNICATION SKILLS

SHERRI MABRY GORDON

Rosen
YA

New York

Published in 2018 by The Rosen Publishing Group, Inc.
29 East 21st Street, New York, NY 10010

Library of Congress Cataloging-in-Publication Data

Names: Gordon, Sherri Mabry, author.
Title: How to create digital portfolios to develop communication skills / Sherri Mabry Gordon.
Description: First edition. | New York, NY : Rosen Publishing, 2018. | Series: Project learning using digital portfolios | Includes bibliographical references and index. | Audience: Grade 7 to 12.
Identifiers: LCCN 2017001579 | ISBN 9781508175308 (library bound book)
Subjects: LCSH: Electronic portfolios in education—Juvenile literature. | Digital media—Juvenile literature. | Communication—Juvenile literature.
Classification: LCC LB1029.P67 G67 2018 | DDC 371.39—dc23
LC record available at https://lccn.loc.gov/2017001579

Manufactured in the United States of America

CONTENTS

In this fast-paced, always-connected world, a digital portfolio can give you an edge. Whether you are competing for a scholarship, applying to college, or looking for a job, a digital portfolio is a wonderful way to tell others who you are and where you are going. Just ask Kara Wellman, a recent graduate of Kent State University and a graphic designer at PPA Graphics in central Ohio, how useful digital portfolios can be.

"When I went in for my job interview at PPA Graphics, they had my portfolio up on a large screen in the conference room," Wellman says. "It was a little intimidating at first to realize that people were actually looking at my work and evaluating me on it."

But she says it was a great tool for communicating with others about her work. As she and the interviewers reviewed the portfolio, she described the process she used in each piece. As a result, her portfolio not only served as a conversation starter, but it also provided a visual element. The interviewers could see and experience her work in a unique way. And in the end, she got the job.

Wellman says she first began experimenting with developing a portfolio in her high school AP art class. But her portfolio, and her work, has evolved a lot since then. She says the same thing will happen for other young people who are just learning how to develop a digital portfolio. What you produce today may not be what you show a future employer, but the process of learning how to showcase your work and organize your thoughts is one that you want to start honing now.

One of the best ways to get started is to experiment with different portfolio tools. "Play around with

Digital portfolios allow people to see and experience your work in a unique way.

the tools, typefaces, and colors and see what works for you, but keep it simple," Wellman suggests. "You want your portfolio to tell others who you are without overwhelming them with a lot of different colors and typefaces."

When people look at your portfolio, they should get a sense of your style, Wellman adds. "They also will be looking to see if you are organized and can communicate well."

What's more, digital portfolios are useful tools for everyone regardless of their interests. For years, people assumed only artists, photographers, designers, and writers needed portfolios. But a portfolio also can be useful for budding scientists, social activists, computer programmers, and countless other professions. Regardless of what you plan to do, portfolios are a great way to showcase your work and communicate with others.

You should discover everything you need to know about building your own digital portfolio so that you can share a little bit of yourself with others. Once you've learned everything you can, you should understand how to implement it to put your best digital foot forward.

CHAPTER ONE

SHOW & TELL: HOW DIGITAL PORTFOLIOS BENEFIT YOU!

Leonardo da Vinci (1452–1519), an artist, inventor, and mathematician, left behind hundreds of journals containing his thoughts, notes, diagrams, and sketches. Although Leonardo is best known for painting the *Mona Lisa*, he was also gifted in many other areas. This fact is evidenced in the notebooks he compiled. Today, these notebooks would be considered his portfolio.

Just as Leonardo's notebooks show the world another side of him, student portfolios increase the depth to which you can communicate about who you are. Suddenly, with a digital portfolio, those around you discover so much more about you. For instance, they might learn that the gifted math student is also actively involved in the community and has a passion for social justice issues.

Another noteworthy example of the value and longevity of portfolios is seen in the collection of work of John Updike (1932–2009). Updike, an author who won the Pulitzer Prize

John Updike, a writer and Pulitzer Prize winner, worked tirelessly to catalog his work, thoughts, and notes. According to his wife, Martha Updike, he considered his collection a representation of him and the times in which he lived.

twice, put together an extensive collection of his thoughts, notes, and other work. Now that he has passed away, this archive is being housed at the Houghton Library at Harvard University.

"The archive was vitally important to him, [especially in his last days]," his wife, Martha Updike, explains. "He saw it not just as a collection of his working materials, but as also a record of the time he lived in."

The same is true for digital portfolios. They can be used to offer a glimpse of your life. Today, students are using digital portfolios in much the same way—to show the world where they have been and where they are going.

In simple terms, a digital portfolio is a collection of your work that can be shared with others online. Ideally, it illustrates your learning and development over time and communicates with others what your interests and passions are, as well as your future goals.

What's more, you can use a digital portfolio to showcase your work and communicate with those around you. Whether it is a conversation with a teacher, another student, or even a college admissions officer, digital portfolios are an excellent tool for sharing insight into your thought processes, as well as the range of your experiences.

YOUR ROADMAP FOR THE FUTURE

One of the benefits of a digital portfolio is the fact that it can be used as a tool for self-reflection. For instance, you can look back at what you have accomplished so far and think about where you are going. Not only will this help you define your interests, but it also will help you come up with new goals.

Digital portfolios are also useful in helping you clarify what direction you want to go with your learning. In fact, they are often a starting point for conversations with other people interested in the same things you are.

"The trend is that everything will be electronic," says Dr. Muriel Gallego, an associate professor of applied linguistics at Ohio University. "Young kids should embrace the idea of a digital portfolio because it will be a great learning experience for them. Some of my students really enjoy it and produce some very beautiful and creative portfolios."

ADVANTAGES AND DISADVANTAGES OF PORTFOLIOS

Overall, creating a digital portfolio has both advantages and disadvantages. Here are some of the advantages according to Dr. Gallego:

- Digital portfolios are easily accessible and portable.
- They are convenient for interviewers.
- Digital portfolios are easily revised over time.
- They show others that you know how to manage and use technology.
- Digital portfolios can include other elements, such as videos.

Digital portfolios are not only useful when applying for a job. They also can be a great tool for self-reflection.

- They increase the size of your audience because they are shared online.

However, there are some disadvantages to digital portfolios. These include:

- Developing and maintaining a digital portfolio can be time-consuming.
- You may still need a hard copy of various items for the interview.
- Some people may be tempted to copy or steal your ideas and your work.
- Not everyone will actually take the time to view your portfolio.

IT'S NEVER TOO EARLY TO THINK ABOUT COLLEGE

Digital portfolios help students keep their accomplishments, their work, their community service, and other activities centralized and organized. In turn, this becomes a valuable resource when the time comes to apply for college.

At Pickerington High School Central, a high school just outside of Columbus, Ohio, the students are equipped with access to Naviance. Naviance is a program aimed at helping students navigate through choices in colleges and careers, explains Julie Brunner, a school counselor and department head.

"Through Naviance, they can explore colleges and careers and take personality assessments," Brunner explains. "They also can create lists of their service projects and create notes to refer to later when they are applying for scholarships or to colleges and universities. These notes are also useful when they need to develop essays."

Although the Naviance system is not technically a digital portfolio, it supports the development of a portfolio in the future. "Through Naviance students can build a résumé, journal, set goals, and keep track of all their assessments," Brunner says. "They also can upload documents and develop a list of colleges they are interested in and match it to the common application. This makes applying to college so much easier for the students."

Students in Pickerington can access Naviance as early as junior high. In fact, experts say that the earlier you begin planning your college application, the better. Even if the

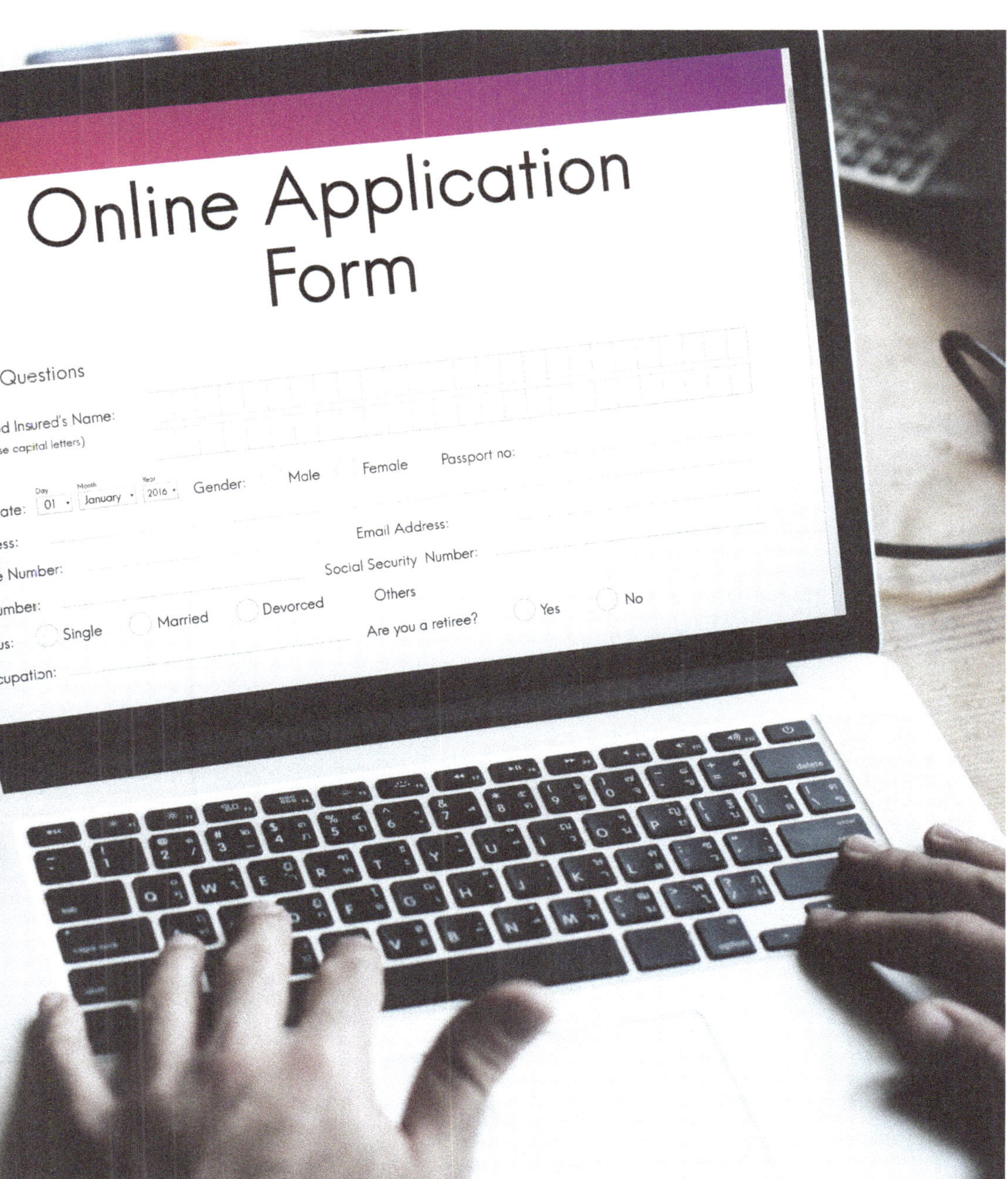

Experts say the sooner you begin planning your college application and essays, the better it will be in the long run. Use your digital portfolio as a tool for keeping all your ideas and accomplishments in one place.

first documents, videos, and other samples you include in the portfolio are never used in a final college application, the process of compiling a digital portfolio will help you start thinking about college. It also improves your critical thinking and your communication skills. The entire process helps you think about what you are doing right now and how it applies to your future goals.

"It [also] reduces stress, if little by little, you learn [how to build your college résumé], rather than waiting until the last couple of weeks to learn to do everything. I think it's a great thing," says Veronica Hauad, deputy dean of admissions at the University of Chicago.

PAPER IS SO LAST YEAR

One of the biggest benefits of a digital portfolio is the ability to get ongoing feedback on your work. For instance, when digital portfolios are used in classrooms, they allow students like you to communicate with one another and collaborate on projects much more quickly.

**BONUS TIP:
DIGITAL PORTFOLIOS HELP YOU ...**

- Showcase your work
- Brand yourself
- Practice digital citizenship
- Develop a sense of belonging
- Provide a sense of authorship
- Boost self-confidence
- Communicate with the world around you

As a result, you can use a portfolio to post drafts of a project and then share them with others. In turn, other students can comment on your work, inclucing offering compliments or helpful suggestions. By comparison, paper documents create a slow process and are not usually very interactive as a digital portfolio.

Digital portfolios also provide a way for people to comment quickly and easily, unlike paper documents, which often lead to one-way communication. Then, you can implement changes that are helpful and ignore those that really do not fit with the goals of the assignment.

Overall, a well-designed digital portfolio gives you an opportunity to chart your growth, your learning, and your activities. It also provides a great way to tell your story. In the end, people who view your portfolio should feel like they know a little more about you.

CHAPTER TWO

NUTS & BOLTS: BUILDING A PORTFOLIO THAT WORKS FOR YOU

Everyone should have a collection of their personal bests—an assortment of their accomplishments and their best work that can be shared easily with others. Today, this collection of work is usually presented in the form of a digital portfolio.

In the beginning stages, your digital portfolio might just be a place where you store your work. But as you mature as a student and collect more materials, it will morph into a space where you showcase your best pieces. Eventually, you will use your portfolio to apply for scholarships, internships, and even college. You also can use your portfolio as a conversation starter with teachers, peers, and people who are interested in the same things you are.

WHY IS THIS PROCESS IMPORTANT?

Over the last few years, digital portfolios have become more important than ever before. For instance, most college admissions

Most colleges expect you to include a digital portfolio with your college application. Start working on yours now so that it looks both polished and professional.

officers expect you to include a digital portfolio with your application. Problems arise, though, if you wait until someone asks for a portfolio before you develop one.

Waiting until the last minute comes at a cost. For instance, if you rush through the process, your portfolio is likely to look disorganized, messy, and unprofessional. There also is a high probability that it will be riddled with mistakes. In the end, a portfolio that is unprofessional communicates a negative message about you.

Do not be that person. Start working on your portfolio now. If you do, you will have an advantage over other students your age. Begin by collecting your best schoolwork, as well as information on your community service activities, your awards and achievements, and your future goals.

HOW DO YOU BENEFIT FROM HAVING A PORTFOLIO?

Portfolios are something every student needs, including you. Here are the top ways you will benefit from preparing a portfolio.

- **You will be prepared to apply for internships, scholarships, and college.**
- **Portfolios help prepare you for communicating clearly.**
- **Well-designed portfolios showcase your accomplishments, abilities, and skills.**
- **Portfolios communicate the results of your projects, work, and service activities.**
- **You will learn how to keep track of and document your achievements and results.**
- **Portfolios help serve as a personal database of your work.**
- **You can use your portfolio to assess your strengths, weaknesses, growth, and progress.**
- **Portfolios allow you to evaluate your own work, including what your preferences are.**

SELECT YOUR COMMUNICATION VEHICLE

There are many free resources for creating your digital portfolio. Here is an overview of some of the most popular tools that are available to you. However, keep in mind that there are many different options out there for creating digital portfolios. If you do not see something on this list that you like, do some research of your own. There are countless resources out there available to you.

- **Google Drive.** This tool helps you create and share your materials. It is also a great storage tool because you can keep all your stuff in one place. From photos, stories, designs, and papers to drawings, recordings, and videos, you can store everything in one central location. Once you upload a file, you can invite people to access it if you want. Google Drive offers you about 15 GB of space for free and is a great tool for kids in middle school who just want to keep all their materials in one place. You can also invite others to view, download, or collaborate on any of your files. So the opportunities for communicating with others are endless.
- **Weebly.** This online platform allows you to create a high-quality site. If you use this resource, you can structure your digital portfolio like a website. Weebly offers both free as well as paid options, depending on what you want your portfolio to accomplish. A pair of college friends who saw how difficult it was for people to put their work online developed Weebly. They wanted everyone to be able to create a high-quality site if they wanted to.
- **Wix.** This online platform allows people to build a high-quality website or digital portfolio at no cost. What's more, you can use this tool to create an online presence, and you do not need to know how to code. According to the company,

it has "the only drag and drop website building platform" around. It also offers more than five hundred templates, hosting services, and lots of features for free.

- **Easy Portfolios.** This is an app that can be downloaded from iTunes. The cost is $1.99, and it allows you to record audio, write text, take photos, and record video directly into a portfolio. You also can import it on Dropbox. Most people use this app to store information that they will later use to develop a portfolio they can share with others. This app would be a good tool for gathering all the samples you will later use for your actual portfolio.

SETTING YOUR DIGITAL COMPASS

Before you can design a solid digital portfolio, you have to know where you are headed. Think about how you want the

There are many different options out there for creating digital portfolios. Take some time to research what is available and pick what is right for you.

portfolio to look, what you want it to say about you, and what you hope to accomplish with the portfolio.

Julie Brunner, a school counselor for Pickerington Local Schools, suggests going through your notes, samples, and lists of

Take some time to plan your portfolio before you develop it. Not only should you consider your goals, but you also should take a look at your materials and determine what items help you put your best digital foot forward.

achievements and reflecting on what you have accomplished and what you hope to accomplish in the future.

It also is helpful to ask yourself: "What are my goals?" This question will help you clarify the direction you want to take with your digital portfolio. Remember, if you don't know what you want to accomplish with your digital portfolio, you won't know if it is working.

Next, it is a good idea to develop the roadmap for your portfolio. Write down what features you want your portfolio to contain, such as an "About Me" section and a "Contact Me" section. You also should think through how you want to showcase your work. Sketch out the links you want in your portfolio and outline what materials you will include.

Kara Wellman, a graphic designer in central Ohio, suggests spending most of your time planning your portfolio. "Look at other digital portfolios

BONUS TIP:
OWN YOUR NAME

If you can, purchase your name as a domain name or a web address. Having a website that says "your-name.com" makes it so much easier for colleges and potential employers to find you. For instance, Kara Wellman, a graphic designer from central Ohio, has a digital portfolio with her name in it. You can find her at karawellman.com.

It is more powerful and looks more professional to have your name as the **URL** instead of your name after a slash or a period. What's more, it is not too expensive to buy a custom domain if you use a site like GoDaddy.com. With sites like that, it may cost less than $10 a year to own your name online. Spending $10 a year on a domain name may even be something that could help you in the long run.

If you can, make sure you own your name. In other words, purchase a URL with your name in it. In the end, it makes it much easier for colleges and universities to find you.

in order to get ideas on what elements you like and do not like," she says. "You also should be sure that your portfolio is structured the way you want it to be before you start building it. It is a lot harder to change the design of your digital portfolio after it is completed."

Just remember, the digital portfolio you build should say a lot about you—even when you are not there to talk about it or walk people through it. Think of it like a display window for your work and accomplishments. People can view it any time. So you want to make sure it represents you well.

CHAPTER THREE

PORTFOLIOS THAT POP: PUTTING YOUR BEST DIGITAL FOOT FORWARD

At first, the thought of communicating to others about who you are might cause you to feel anxious. After all, you are sharing a piece of yourself with the world. You are adding photos, videos, and words and allowing others to draw conclusions and opinions about you and your work.

But it doesn't have to be scary, especially if you take time to really think about what information you want to share. What's more, it is your portfolio and you are in control of the message. If done properly, you should be able to change and update your portfolio at any time. This way, your portfolio always looks fresh and relevant.

Sometimes, putting together a portfolio can seem overwhelming. But it doesn't have to be. With proper planning, it can be a fun experience to share a little of yourself with others.

GETTING STARTED

Your teen years are some of the most exciting—and the most overwhelming—years of your life. One minute you may feel self-confident and in control, and the next minute you may feel insecure and unsure of where you are headed. But all of these feelings are normal. What's more, this roller coaster of emotions you regularly feel can give you insight into where you are headed and what you want to accomplish in life.

According to Kara Wellman, you should take some time to reflect on who you are and the message you want to convey. Think about your goals, the work you want to showcase, and the message you want to send to your target audience.

Remember, first impressions are important. When someone looks at your digital portfolio, you want this person to like what he or she sees. Aside from showcasing your best work, your portfolio design is important. Your goal should be to keep it simple and elegant. Do not overcomplicate things by trying to stuff too much material into your portfolio, Wellman suggests.

Dr. Gallego agrees. "Try not to overload readers visually," she suggests. "Pay attention to the type of font and the colors you choose. For instance, avoid using a rainbow of colors. And make sure it is consistent throughout."

CHOOSING YOUR BEST WORK

Most experts recommend showcasing anywhere from seven to ten samples that demonstrate what you have done. Overall, look for pieces that highlight your best work.

Ideally, these pieces should not be more than five years old. There are some exceptions to this rule, though. If you completed a big project that still looks current and it received an

KEY POINTS TO REMEMBER

- People have limited attention spans. Be selective with what you include.
- Ninety percent of the information our brain processes is visual. Make sure your digital portfolio is visually appealing.
- Even if the work you have done is not visual in nature, you still need a digital portfolio. Look for ways to provide a visual element, such as including graphics or photos from brainstorming sessions or the process behind the work.
- Remember, less is more. Watch that your portfolio does not become too busy looking.
- The best portfolios are easy to navigate. Consider using categories, links, and other resources that are easy to follow and make sense to a first-time user.
- People want to know the person behind the work. Make sure you take time to let people know who you are, your thought processes, or your philosophy.

award or two, it is fine to include it in your portfolio, especially if it is polished and serves your purpose.

When trying to decide which pieces to showcase first, start off with your best piece of work, Wellman says. "Your portfolio should lead with your best work and finish with your second best piece of work. Basically, you want to start strong and end strong."

Your digital portfolio samples should also:

- Communicate your strengths, your experience, as well as the variety of things you have worked on.
- Look fresh, new, and recent; old samples can look tired and outdated.
- Be appealing and easily tailored to fit the needs of the person or audience you are trying to communicate with.
- Fit into clear categories; remember, categories make it easier for people to search through your portfolio for things that apply to them.
- Be consistent; your digital portfolio design should match your personal style and look like it is part of your résumé and your other application materials.
- Create a visually appealing experience for your target audience; know who will be looking at your portfolio and tailor it to what you would like for them to see and know about you.

Finally, Wellman suggests that you really look at your samples critically and carefully. Select the ones that not only show others who you are and what you can do, but also highlight your best work. If you are having trouble deciding which pieces to eliminate from your portfolio, Wellman recommends getting a second opinion.

"Don't feel pressured to put every single thing you have done online," she says. "Choose your best work and curate that. Ultimately, your portfolio is only as good as your weakest piece. It can be hard to eliminate pieces because you might feel a connection to it, but ultimately you only want your best work out there."

BONUS TIP: SUCCESSFUL DIGITAL PORTFOLIOS HAVE THESE FIVE THINGS IN COMMON

- The best digital portfolios make good use of white space and have a clean, uncluttered feel to them.
- Effective digital portfolios clearly communicate who the person is, including what type of work the person has done.
- The samples of work are well organized and easy to navigate.
- In a solid digital portfolio, it is not hard to figure out how to contact the person whose work is being presented.
- The best digital portfolios are easy to update when materials become outdated.

WRITE A STRONG "ABOUT ME" SECTION

The goal of this section is to really sell yourself, your skills, and your experience. However, you want to keep it simple and conversational at the same time. To do this, try writing it as if you were talking to a friend. You want your bio to make you sound approachable. You can also showcase your awards and achievements in this section. Or, you can create a special section for your awards, especially if you have been recognized a lot.

Wellman suggests writing your "About Me" section in first person. In other words, you would start a sentence with "I." On

Wellman's portfolio, she kept the description short and simple, using short blurbs to give the reader insight into her personality without overloading them with information. For instance, her "About Me" section begins with the following blurbs: "Detail oriented. Dog person. Lover of people, carbs, and typography." As a reader, you get a clear picture of who she is without a lot of extra words.

Meanwhile, Dr. Gallego says that some "About Me" sections require students to provide a more formal description of who they are. For instance, most of her students are either continuing their education or looking for teaching positions. As a result, they tend not to include much personal information in the "About Me" section, especially if their portfolio contains a section with their teaching philosophy. Visitors to their digital

Every digital portfolio should have a strong "About Me" section. Take some time to reflect on what you want to tell the world about yourself.

portfolios will get a clear understanding of who the students are by reading that section and do not need a long "About Me" section.

"When you are trying to decide what to include in your 'About Me' section, review what others have done to see what style you like best," Dr. Gallego suggests. "This section can be very challenging to write. Kids often do not think about who they are. So they have to do some soul searching in order to know what to highlight."

She also points out that too many times, young people think they have to look perfect and put too much pressure on themselves. "Colleges are not looking for the perfect student," she says. "Instead, they are looking for a student that can build on personal experiences and be a critical thinker. They are looking for kids that can notice their imperfections and think about how they can improve."

MAKE IT EASY FOR PEOPLE TO CONTACT YOU

The whole point of a digital portfolio is to get people to interact with you about your work. Ultimately, you want to talk with them. But that cannot happen if you do not make it easy for them to get in touch with you. As a result, be sure to include information about how to contact you. For instance, you might want to create an email address specifically for your digital

portfolio. Another option is to create a contact form on your digital portfolio. Or, you could suggest that people contact you through your school.

Remember, it is not a good idea for you to include addresses or telephone numbers. Doing so presents too much of a safety concern. There are many people in this world who pretend to

Remember, the purpose of your portfolio is to start conversations with others about your work, your passions, and your goals. Be sure you take time to share your work with others.

be people they are not. And you do not want these people to know personal information about you. Instead, talk to your parents about the best way to develop a contact page.

Some students choose to have their digital portfolio password-protected. This way, only people they authorize to view the portfolio can see the information that is out there. This adds another layer of security to the portfolio.

But whatever route you decide to take, do not develop a digital portfolio and then never share it with anyone. The entire purpose of a portfolio is to start conversations with others about your work. Your portfolio should be the vehicle that allows you to connect and communicate with others around you.

CHAPTER FOUR

DIGITAL DIALOGUES: HOW TO START CONVERSATIONS THAT PROMOTE YOUR PORTFOLIO

Everything you post online tells a story about who you are to outsiders. This story then becomes your digital footprint. When you are young, it may not seem like a big deal, but it is. Online posts have a longer shelf life than you may realize.

Do an internet search of your name, or a friend's name. What did you find? You probably found references of awards or accomplishments. Maybe you found something that you or your friend didn't want the world to see. Remember, when something is posted online you lose some control over it and it can be out there

Everything you post online tells a story about who you are. Be sure the story you are telling college recruiters and potential employers is a positive one.

for years to come. As a result, your goal should be to make sure the things people read about you are positive. This task is accomplished by managing your online reputation.

CONTROLLING YOUR WEB PRESENCE OR YOUR ONLINE REPUTATION

To gauge what your online presence is like, try doing a web search of your own name. Type in your first and last name, along with your city and state. Then start reading. What types of things are out there? Is there anything you would find embarrassing if you knew your grandmother was reading it? What do you think a college admissions officer would think of the things online?

Maintaining a positive online reputation is a crucial part of making your digital portfolio successful. Done correctly, it will help elevate your portfolio and increase the likelihood that people want to check it out. As a result, it is always a good idea to look at social media and blogs as tools to build your web presence and communicate with others. Meanwhile, avoid using them to rant about pet peeves, engage in digital drama, and post silly photos and videos. Here are some guidelines to managing your online reputation.

- **Join Social Networking Sites Like LinkedIn.** Not many students utilize LinkedIn, but it is one of the most useful tools for promoting your skills and your digital portfolio. Through LinkedIn, you can showcase your résumé, link to your digital portfolio, and network with others.

For instance, students often connect with admissions officers through the university pages on LinkedIn. When you

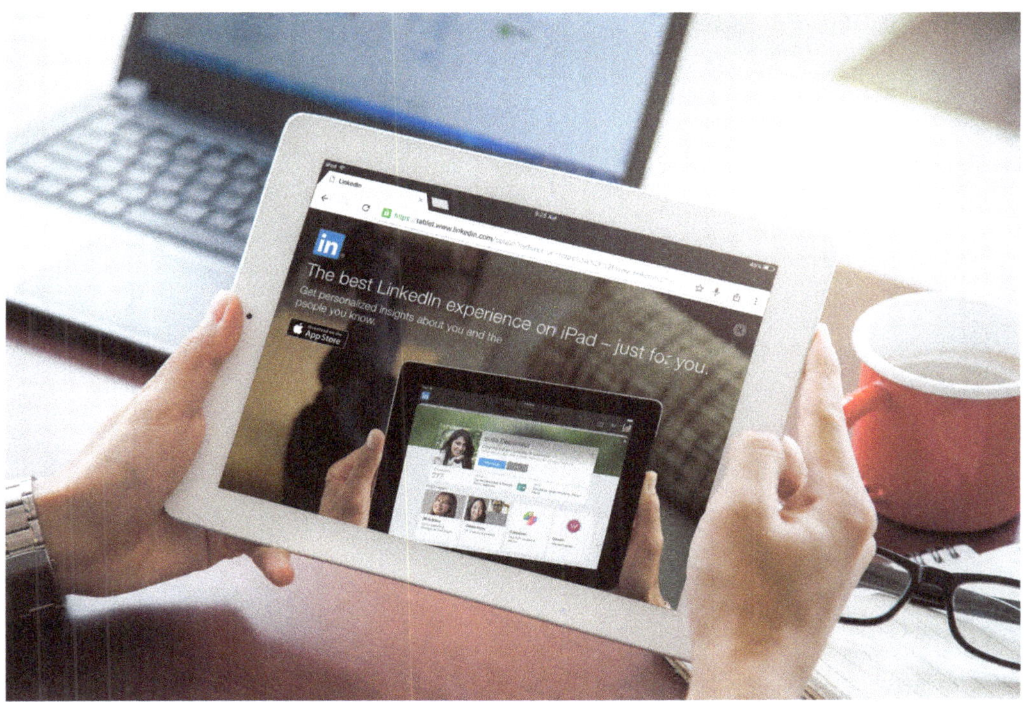

It is important to maintain a positive online reputation. Look at everything you do online as a way to build your online presence and leave behind a positive digital footprint.

take the initiative to connect with college admissions, this is referred to as "demonstrated interest" and it speaks volumes about your interest in the university. Suddenly, you become what they consider a serious candidate for the college and you have an avenue for getting your digital portfolio in front of them.

- **Publish Quality Content.** If you are planning to develop a blog or make videos on YouTube, be sure that they are not only high quality and useful, but that they also relate in some way to your digital portfolio.

Another option is to use these tools to promote a cause you are passionate about. Not only does activity like this show initiative and creativity, but it also helps you build your platform online—and it looks great on a college application. Just be sure to include links to these things on your digital portfolio. You want to encourage communication about your projects as much as possible.

What's more, experts explain that the more high-quality content you produce, the better your chances are that it will out-rank any negative content that is found online. In other words, the good content can push the negative stuff low enough in the search results that no one sees it.

- **Manage the Content That Is Out There.** If you see content online that is negative or you feel doesn't communicate good things about you, contact the person who posted it to see if he or she will remove it. If the message is particularly damaging, you can contact the social media site where it is posted. Sites like Instagram and Facebook pay particular attention to anything that is negative about minors.

Remember, your online reputation is a valuable asset. If it is managed appropriately, it can help open doors and start conversations. Focus on building a solid reputation now and you will have a head start on success.

STARTING A DIGITAL DIALOGUE

There are a number of audiences for your portfolio, including teachers, classmates, coaches, college admissions officers, and more. But are you reaching them with the best possible information? Here are some tips for starting a dialogue.

TIPS FOR KEEPING TABS ON YOUR ONLINE REPUTATION

Online reputation management is not an easy task, especially if there are a lot of references to you online that do not paint the picture you want them to. But it can be done with a little hard work.

Begin by keeping track of what others are posting. You can either sign up through Google to be notified every time your name is mentioned online, or you can do a search once a month to check for questionable posts about you.

If you find something you do not like, send requests to social media networks or the website administrators to have any questionable content removed. Most social media sites will investigate posts, especially those that involve minors. If you stay on top of what is being posted about you, in the end you will be successful at maintaining a positive online reputation.

Be sure to strategically think about and plan your posts. The goal is to be strategic with your online posts and blogs. Make sure what you are posting ties in with the things you are passionate about or relates to your career goals.

For instance, one high school student that aspires to be an author some day writes online reviews about young adult books. Then, she tweets about the books and directs people to her blog. As a result of her efforts, she has a large following on Twitter and has a variety of online conversations with authors, publishers, and agents.

Use social media to your advantage. Be sure to post any awards and honors you receive.

Not only is she providing a service by sharing her thoughts on books, but she is also building a platform for herself in the process. What's more, people are familiar with her name and more willing to discuss her work because of how she has managed her online presence.

You can also use social media to your advantage. If you receive an award, achieve a goal, or reach a milestone, post it on your social media account. Not only do these types of posts complement your digital portfolio, but you can also use them to point interested people to your portfolio.

If you feel like posting this information about yourself is bragging, ask a parent or a sibling to post about it and tag you in the post. The idea is to flood the internet with positive information about your accomplishments, sports activities, service projects, and clubs. By doing so, these positive things will be the first to pop up when a college recruiter, coach, or prospective employer searches your name.

BONUS TIP: KNOW YOUR PORTFOLIO

After you have completed your portfolio, make sure you become familiar with it. Practice how you plan to share your portfolio with others. Talk through your beliefs, qualifications, and experiences. Doing so helps you become better prepared when the time comes to present it to a teacher, a friend, or a potential employer.

Pay attention to what is trending online and use these trends to help promote your content.

BE AWARE OF TRENDING TOPICS

One final thought on how to generate attention for your digital portfolio and start a conversation with others is to be aware of trending topics online. Most young people like you want to have a presence online. The goal is to gain a large number of views, likes, or friends. But the key is to do this responsibly.

For instance, when you comment on a hot topic online, make sure your posts are fair, well thought out, and respectful. Everything you publish should be meaningful in some way. It also should connect to your platform and your goals. You also want to direct attention to your digital portfolio anytime that you can.

Remember, with every post you make, you are leaving a permanent footprint online. As a result, you want the impression you leave to be a lasting one.

CHAPTER FIVE

REAL, RELEVANT & READY: KEEPING YOUR PORTFOLIO CURRENT

No matter what grade you are in, keeping your portfolio fresh and relevant is a key part of your future success. You never know when an opportunity will present itself. For instance, you might strike up a conversation with someone in the library or at a coffee shop and want to show them what you have done. Or maybe your new teacher wants to see what types of things you have done in the past. But if you do not have a current digital portfolio, what you show them may be old and outdated.

"One of the great things about digital portfolios is that you can pull it up on your phone and show someone some of your work," says Kara Wellman. "People also want to be able to Google your name and find your work. So if your portfolio is not functional and not a good indicator of your work, then that is a bad reflection on you."

For this reason, experts recommend adding fresh work as it is completed. "Your portfolio should always be a work in progress," says Julie Brunner. "You want to continue to add information as it

Make sure you are updating your portfolio on a regular basis. You never know when someone will want to see your work.

becomes available. If you wait until you need it, you have waited too long. It can be very time-consuming to add work to a portfolio. So take the time to do it as it becomes available, rather than trying to assemble everything at one time."

MAKE RELEVANCE AND READINESS A PRIORITY

When it comes to keeping your digital portfolio up to date and relevant, it is very easy to procrastinate or put it off because you feel like you just do not have the time. For this reason, experts recommend that you set aside a little time each week or a couple times a month to polish your portfolio. It is just like anything else in life. You have to schedule time to make it happen. So pick a few days each month where you will spend an hour or two working on your portfolio. Then follow through on your commitment.

Just like exercising or eating right, if you make a commitment to do a little bit each day, you are more likely to stay on track. But if you let it go for months at a time, before you know it you are not where you want to be. The same is true for your portfolio. If you make time for it, your portfolio will stay fresh and current. And when you need it, it will be ready to go.

SEVEN THINGS TEENS SHOULD NEVER POST ONLINE

If you are like most teens, you probably do not put much thought into what you post online. After all, you probably have set up decent privacy settings and assume only your friends can see what you post. But that is not always the case.

You need to remember that once you post something online, you lose some control of it. People can copy your posts or take photos of them and share them in more public places. For this reason, you need to be very careful about what you put online, especially if you want your digital portfolio to be taken seriously. Here are seven things you should never post online.

- **Personal Information.** When you post personal details like your address, phone number, and birthday, you are putting yourself at risk for things like identity theft and cyberbullying. Another risk is that an online predator will contact you.
- **Inappropriate Photos.** Make sure all the photos you share online communicate a consistent message. You do not want to post something inappropriate and then expect people to take your portfolio seriously.
- **Rude Comments.** Good digital citizens treat people with respect online. Make sure your comments are positive and uplifting.
- **Pranks or Jokes.** Posting inappropriate jokes or off-color comments does not portray a good online image.
- **Personal Problems.** It is always best to resolve personal problems in person. Refrain from posting about fights with friends or disagreements with others online.
- **Details About Plans.** When you share information about where you will be or what you will be doing, you are putting yourself at risk. This information makes it easier for people to take advantage of you.
- **Rumors or Gossip.** Aside from the fact that it is not appropriate to spread gossip or discuss rumors, posting them online is even worse. It is best to avoid this type of communication at all costs.

LOOK FOR WAYS TO PROMOTE YOUR WORK

What good is a portfolio if no one ever sees your work? For this reason, look for ways to promote your work online. One way you can get your work noticed is through social media. The key, according to Austin Kleon, author of *Show Your Work!*, is to continuously share your work, even if you think it is not perfect or finished. But you also want to avoid oversharing as well. You do not want people to start to see your posts and information as spam. So you need to find a balance between promoting your work online and the other posts you might share.

Another option for sharing your work is to write a blog. Your blog should be about something that is of interest to you. You can share your thoughts, feelings, and passions in short articles that you can then share on social media. Throughout the blog,

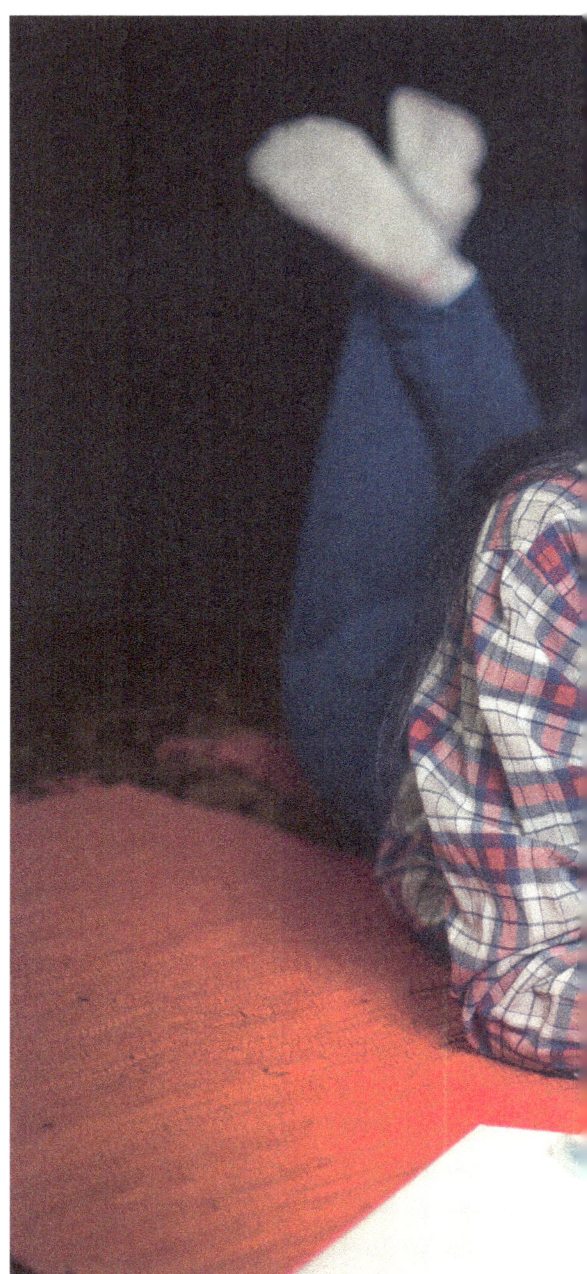

Look for ways to promote and share your work online. Remember, the goal is to communicate with others what you have to offer.

you can reference your digital portfolio or share items from it. If you allow people to comment on your blog, you have an easy avenue for talking with others about things you care about.

Other options for getting your digital portfolio in front of people include making videos, taking photographs, and participating in contests. The key is to find ways to keep your work out there in front of others. This helps build awareness of who you are and what you have accomplished.

BE CONSISTENT

Meanwhile, Dr. Gallego suggests that you make sure that all the information you put online sends a consistent message about who you are. "You don't want to post really crazy things on social media and then try to have a very professional portfolio. The two things contradict each other and your message is lost."

Instead, she advises that young people learn early how to post responsibly online. Learning how to curate information, or pick and choose what you will share, is a really important skill. Make sure what you are posting online is appropriate and communicating the message you want it to.

BE REAL

Because most communication that takes place online is done from behind a keyboard, it is very tempting for young people to pretend to be someone they are not. While it is important to put your best digital foot forward, make sure it is actually your footprint you are leaving behind. In other words, be truthful about who you are and what you have accomplished.

BONUS TIP: WRITE LIKE YOU SPEAK

Successful "About Me" sections sound like the person they are describing. Resist the urge to use words that you would not normally use. Instead, select words that you use on a regular basis. What's more, Wellman suggests writing in first person because readers feel like you are talking directly to them. After writing this section, if you still feel like it is too stiff or does not reflect who you truly are, try recording yourself first. Pretend like you are talking to someone about the things you enjoy. Once you are done, you can transcribe that information and help craft an authentic "About Me" section.

One place where you might be tempted to embellish a little is the "About Me" section. But this section is where you can truly embrace who you are and share it with others. If you do not like coffee, do not say that you do in the "About Me" section just because you think it sounds cool or hip. Instead, share things that show people who you truly are.

If those things change in a year or two, be sure to update your "About Me" section. Remember, this section is often the most-read part of a digital portfolio, so make sure you keep it up to date. This section also serves as a great conversation starter, especially if the person reading it has similar interests.

Make sure you ask others for their opinion on your digital portfolio. They might be able to provide suggestions on ways to improve it.

WHAT'S NEXT?

It's also a good idea to get feedback on your portfolio on a regular basis. Ask others to look at it and give you their thoughts. Ask them: Is it hard to follow or easy to read? Does it sound and look like me? Does it communicate the image I want it to?

Keep in mind that digital portfolios are constantly evolving and changing, just as you grow and change. As a result, you need to look at your portfolio as a work in progress and not a completed project. Be sure you are not only taking steps to update and improve it, but that you are also sharing it with others.

While there is no guarantee that your digital portfolio will get you into the college of your choice or land you the job of your dreams, it is a vital tool that you want to have in your arsenal. A solidly crafted portfolio that is current and fresh will definitely give you an advantage over someone who either has a poorly developed portfolio or none at all. Remember, the purpose of a digital portfolio is to help you put your best digital foot forward. What you accomplish with that is up to you.

GLOSSARY

college admissions officer A person responsible for finding students that fit a college's requirements and standards.

demonstrated interest When a young person takes the initiative and contacts a college admissions office.

digital drama Conflict that occurs online.

digital footprint The mark that a person leaves online in the way of social media posts, blogs, websites, portfolios, and more; articles written about the person also contribute to the digital footprint.

digital portfolio A collection of work that can be shared with others online.

domain name A street address for the World Wide Web; it is the name of a website that makes it easy to find it on the internet; karawellman.com is an example of a domain name.

internship A job that high school and college students have in their field of study; it can be paid or unpaid and is designed to prepare them for work in the field once they graduate.

minor A child who is under the age of eighteen.

online reputation How a person is viewed online based on social media posts, articles, websites, and other online information that mentions the person.

pet peeve A minor annoyance that can cause a person to become frustrated.

Pulitzer Prize An award that recognizes writers for their achievements in the United States.

reputation management The attempt to manage a person's online reputation by posting positive things and deleting negative things.

scholarship Money received to help pay for college that is usually awarded based on grades or athletic abilities; recipients are not expected to repay this money as one would a college loan.

social media A broad term used to describe websites like Facebook, Instagram, Pinterest, and Twitter; these sites are usually used to promote and share content and involve an online community of friends and followers.

social networking The use of social media to communicate informally with other members of a website; usually photos, comments, and videos are shared online.

URL Stands for Uniform Resource Locator; it identifies an address for a page on the internet.

white space A design term that refers to blank space on a page.

Association for Women in Communications
1717 E. Republic Road, Suite A
Springfield, MO 65804
(417) 886-8606
Website: http://www.womcom.org
The Association for Women in Communications believes that
   all communications disciplines are important and should be
   mastered. These disciplines include everything from print
   and broadcast journalism to graphic design and photography.

Common Sense Media
San Francisco Headquarters
650 Townsend, Suite 435
San Francisco, CA 94103
(415) 863-0600
Website: https://www.commonsensemedia.org
Common Sense Media is a nonprofit organization that helps kids
   navigate media and technology. It provides unbiased information, advice, and tools that help kids understand and use media
   and technology responsibly.

Digital Marketing Association
207 Regent Street
London, England W1B 3HH
United Kingdom
Website: https://www.dmaglobal.com
The Digital Marketing Association is a group that offers profes-
   sionals in digital marketing useful information and courses. It
   also offers industry updates and professional support to its
   members.

Digital Media Academy
718 University Avenue, Suite 1100
Los Gatos, CA
(866) 656-3342
Website: https://www.digitalmediaacedemy.org
Digital Media Academy is a leader in tech education for kids,
    teens, and adults. It focuses on building technical skills and
    empowering kids to become lifelong learners in the areas of
    technology and media.
International Communication Association
1500 21st Street NW
Washington, DC 20036
(202) 955-1444
Website: https://www.icahdq.org
The goal of the International Communication Association is
    to promote the study of human communication. One way
    it accomplishes this is by participating in academic research
    worldwide.

National Communication Association
1765 N Street NW
Washington, DC 20036
(202) 464-4622
Website: http://www.natcom.org
The National Communication Association (NCA) promotes
    the importance of all types of communication in public and
    private life. The NCA also believes that quality communica-
    tion can be used to solve problems and improve the quality
    of life.

Pathbrite c/o Engage Learning
500 Terry A. Francois Boulevard, 2nd Floor

San Francisco, CA 94158
(415) 766-4505
Website: https://pathbrite.com
Pathbrite is a cloud-based portfolio platform. By using Pathbrite, users can showcase what they have created, achieved, and mastered. They also can use their materials to communicate with others.

WEBSITES

Because of the changing nature of internet links, Rosen Publishing has developed an online list of websites related to the subject of this book. This site is updated regularly. Please use this link to access the list:

http://www.rosenlinks.com/PROJL/communicate

Blumsack, Larry. *Face-to-Face Is the Ultimate Social Media.* Belmont, MA: Zoka Institute, LLC, 2010.

Fromm, Megan. *Digital Content Creation.* New York, NY: Rosen Publishing, 2015.

Fromm, Megan. *Gathering and Sharing Digital Information.* New York, NY: Rosen Publishing, 2015.

Haggerty, Teri. *Your Key, Your Door: Life Purpose Discovery Book for Teens.* Pensacola, FL: Doorknob Books, 2012.

Landau, Jennifer. *The Right Words: Know What to Say and How to Say It.* New York, NY: Publishing, 2011.

Muchnick, Justin Ross. *Teens' Guide to College & Career Planning, 12th Edition.* Lincoln, NE: Peterson's, 2016.

Newport, Cal. *How to Be a High School Superstar: A Revolutionary Plan to Get into College by Standing Out (Without Burning Out).* New York, NY: Three Rivers Press, 2010.

Roza, Greg. *Listen Up: Communicating with Confidence.* New York, NY: Rosen Publishing, 2012.

Weinick, Suzanne. *Professional Connections.* New York, NY: Rosen Publishing, 2011.

Yearling, Tricia. *How Do I Use Social Networking?* New York, NY: Enslow Publishing, 2015.

BIBLIOGRAPHY

"6 Easy Steps to Create a Successful Online Portfolio." Creative Boom, February 18, 2015. http://www.creativeboom.com/tips/six-easy-steps-to-create-a-successful-online-portfolio.

"A Safe Place for Your Files." Google Drive. https://www.google.com/drive.

Brunner, Julie. Interview with author, October 2016.

Creative Group. "3 Digital Portfolio Best Practices," Robert Half, January 4, 2016. https://www.roberthalf.com/creativegroup/blog/3-digital-portfolio-best-practices-how-to-make-a-portfolio-that-pops.

Frost, Aja. "4 Secrets to Building a Portfolio That Will Make Everyone Want to Hire You." The Muse. https://www.themuse.com/advice/4-secrets-to-building-a-portfolio-thatll-make-everyone-want-to-hire-you.

Gallego, Muriel, Ph.D. Interview with author, October 2016.

GDC Team. "How Do Digital Portfolios Help Students?" Global Digital Citizen, March 2015. https://globaldigitalcitizen.org/how-do-digital-portfolios-help-students.

Gordon, Sherri. "6 Tips on Managing Teen Online Reputations." VeryWell.com, February 15, 2016. https://www.verywell.com/tips-on-managing-your-teens-online-reputation-460576.

Gordon, Sherri. "7 Things Teens Should Never Post on Social Media." VeryWell.com, November 30, 2015. https://www.verywell.com/things-teens-should-never-post-on-social-media-460660.

Grose, Jessica. "The Art of Promotion: 6 Tips for Getting Your Work Discovered." *Fast Company*, March 17, 2014. https://www.fastcocreate.com/3027752/the-art-of-self-promotion-6-tips-for-getting-your-work-discovered.

"How to Create a Digital Portfolio." Washington and Lee University. https://www.wlu.edu/career-development /students/professional-online-presence/digital-portfolios -and-professional-websites/how-to-create-a-digital-portfolio.

"How to Improve Your Digital Footprint for College." Safe Smart Social, September 21, 2016. https://safesmartsocial.com /digital-footprint-college.

Korbey, Holly. "What Will Digital Portfolios Mean for College-Bound Students?" KQED Mind/Shift, March 22, 2016. https:// ww2.kqed.org/mindshift/2016/03/22/what-will-digital -portfolios-mean-for-college-bound-students.

Tanenhaus, Sam. "John Updike's Archive: A Great Writer at Work." *New York Times*, June 20, 2010. http://www.nytimes. com/2010/06/21/books/21updike.html?_r=2>.

Wellman, Kara. Interview with author, October 2016.

ABOUT THE AUTHOR

Sherri Mabry Gordon's passion is to provide young people with information about issues and interests that impact their lives. As a result, nearly all of her books deal with relevant issues like bullying, public shaming, technology, food allergies, and many others. Gordon also is the bullying prevention expert for VeryWell.com. Currently, she is working on several young adult fiction books and writing regularly about bullying for VeryWell.

PHOTO CREDITS

Cover Klaus Vedfelt/DigitalVision/Getty Images; pp. 5, 12–13, 31 Rawpixel.com/Shutterstock.com; p. 8 The Washington Post/Getty Images; p. 10 Randy Miramontez/Shutterstock.com; p. 17 Undrey/Shutterstock.com; pp. 20–21 Bloomberg/Getty Images; pp. 22–23 Vitchanan Photography/Shutterstock.com; p. 24 alex skopje/Shutterstock.com; p. 26 GOLFX/Shutterstock.com; pp. 32–33 pixelheadphoto digitalskillet/Shutterstock.com; p. 35 Syda Productions/Shutterstock.com; p. 37 I AM NIKOM/Shutterstock.com; p. 40 © iStockphoto.com/LuckyBusiness; pp. 42–43 tanuha2001/Shutterstock.com; p. 45 © iStockphoto.com/media photos; pp. 48-49 © iStockphoto.com/gordana jovanovic; pp. 52–53 © iStockphoto.com/kristian sekulic; back cover Alexandr III/Shutterstock.com; interior pages graphic, pp. 7, 16, 26, 35 Ron Dale/Shutterstock.com.

Design: Michael Moy
Editor and Photo Researcher: Ellina Litmanovich